The Life and Good Times of The Rolling Stones

The Life and Good Times of The Rolling Stones

The Life
and Good Times
of The
Rolling Stones

Philip Norman

HARMONY BOOKS/
NEW YORK

Designed by Paul Bowden

Picture research by Susan Ready

Copyright © 1989 by Philip Norman

Photographs copyright © copyright owners, see page 128

Published by Harmony Books, a division of Crown Publishers,
Inc., 225 Park Avenue South, New York, New York 10003

Originally published in Great Britain by Century Hutchinson Ltd.

Harmony and colophon are trademarks of Crown Publishers, Inc.

Printed and bound in Spain by Cayfosa, Barcelona

Library of Congress Cataloging-in-Publication Data
ISBN 0-517-57464-0
10 9 8 7 6 5 4 3 2 1
First American Edition

Introduction

The 1985 Live Aid concert — that ages-overdue birth of humane sensibility in Pop — struck only one regrettable note in its marathon itinerary. This occurred when Bob Dylan took the stage, accompanied by Keith Richards and Ronnie Wood of The Rolling Stones. It soon became clear that Richards and Wood were in a condition which only the most devoted Stones fan of the mid-Seventies would have considered appropriate. Unsteady on old-fashioned boot-heels, raddled faces confused, skinny forearms cluelessly pumping scrub-board guitars, they appeared less like Rock immortals than a pair of disreputable charwomen half-heartedly washing out some socks.

The music was abysmal, but still worse the archaic Gauloise and Jack Daniels reek of the musicians on an afternoon dedicated to altruism and higher thought. To the Live Aid masses, in their conspicuous virtue and wholesome Street-Cred undress, the whole concept of Rolling Stones suddenly seemed ludicrous, if not vaguely obscene. The two bespangled old reprobates were all but laughed off the stage.

As the Nineties dawn, and Pop prepares for its next great leap, the question can even more pertinently be asked. Should anyone but misty-eyed Sixties nostalgics care about The Rolling Stones? What now for that arrogant sub-title their name has borne, unchallenged, through almost three decades? Would you still believe, The World's Greatest Rock 'n' Roll Band?

As usual, do not expect clarification of anything from Mick Jagger. The most potent performer Rock music ever knew has opted for the bland, safe life of an international celebrity. For years his only occupation has been that of keeping himself fashionable: swanning between his French château and his New York town house, or peeping at paparazzi from under Cecil Beaton-ish hat-brims on Mustique. With millions to spend and the world at his feet, he is still plagued by his old paradoxical worm of caution and indecision, somehow never quite acting in that great film, writing that good book or producing significant music on his own. An ageing Nureyev, surrounded by beautiful daughters now as well as paramours, he seems fated to remain a figure of promise all his life.

The soul of the band, as well as its calculating brain, has become infected by celebrity-itis. Keith Richards, since his gaffe at Live Aid, is to be seen less and less in his old gipsy rags and more and more in black designer suits and white silk shirts, albeit open nearly to the waist. That the public can grow accustomed to any face is proved by the increasing prevalence of Keith's ruined physiognomy on TV documentaries and chat shows, as familiar and homely a horror as Grandpa in *The Munsters*. He is off the Most Wanted list, and available to model costume jewellery in glossy magazines.

They are all getting so old. Dear God! Charlie Watts, with his backswept silver hair and Mount Rushmore profile, looks like someone who might have known Paganini. Bill Wyman — by supreme irony, the decade's most scandal-ridden Stone — is within sight of his state pension. Even Ronnie Wood, 'baby' of the ensemble, presents so utterly outmoded a figure, one half expects the Arts Council to declare his brand of late Sixties looning an endangered English craft, perhaps even making some grant to keep up his spiky hair, blue denim pygmy frame and Navajo bangles as part of our national folk heritage.

As a supergroup, they leave behind remarkably few monuments. Their albums are not highly rated, being dismissed — unfairly or not — as pale imitations of The Beatles'. Their films, mostly unreleased, lie in mouldering cans on forgotten shelves. The body of their work, such as it is, can be found on that dusty relic, the 45 r.p.m. 'single'.

Nor have they worked assiduously, like other Sixties Golden Oldies, to keep themselves fresh and current. They have not produced a classic song for something like seventeen years. When they last toured, in 1981 — 2, many of the concerts were an ill-rehearsed shambles. Their last chart hit 'Start Me Up', eight years ago, was even then considered a twilight-time fluke.

Just what is it about these five ageing, social climbing millionaires who individually would seem not to embody much more danger and lawlessness than a copy of *The Highway Code?* Why was it that, when their leader-cum-managing director roused himself, took off his Cecil Beaton hat and announced he was in training again, the same old shiver of half-fearful joy still ran up the spine of two continents?

The Stones were the Sixties incarnate. Granted, The Beatles had more original talent, and more millions of fans. Yet as a contemporary presence, they were strangely vague and insubstantial. Their vast fame somehow dehumanised them, changing beings of flesh and blood to characters in a world-obsessing strip cartoon. The Stones, by contrast, were never other than utterly real, feet on the ground, exploiting the magical times for all they were worth. Many similes have been used for Mick Jagger's mouth as an emblem of the Stones' career. To me, it resembles the jaws of an angler fish, torpidly propped open for whatever, and whoever, might swim inside. An age in history, of a sort, can be recalled as courses from that stupendous feast.

Only for a few months in 1963 were The Beatles anything like a threat or disruption to British society. No sooner had they become a hit group than their manager, Brian Epstein, abetted by Paul McCartney, began steering them along the path of conventional showbiz already wearily trodden by the luckless Elvis Presley. The galvanisers of Britain's youth were remodelled into four cuddly dolls, with no sharp edges or protruding wires, suitable for the whole family.

The first, ghastly social crime of The Stones was simply to reject and ridicule everything Beatle-ish. A group that refused to wear uniform shiny suits onstage or smile cheekily for photographers! A group that abused the privilege of the mop-top fringe, allowing their hair to curl down past their ears and over their stacked-up collars! Horror of all horrors, a group that refused to ride on the revolving stage at the conclusion of ITV's *Sunday Night at the London Palladium!*

From there on, British teenage life could be seen as something more than just an amorphous mass of fringes and corduroy. There were nice, well-behaved teenagers, who appreciated charm and melody, and there were nasty, unruly teenagers, who scowled and mocked and wanted to smash chairs. It became a cultural question as basic as between Montague and Capulet. 'Who do you like? The Beatles or The Stones?'

The myth of good boys versus bad boys, hugely profitable to all, was pure PR myth. The winsome Beatles actually were red-blooded Scousers, with a vivid history of drunkenness, promiscuity and social disease, who continued to do fairly nasty things behind the monastery wall of Brian Epstein's management. The insurgent Stones were well brought-up middle class boys from the London suburbs, until lately sworn to quasi-Marxist penury and altruism. It was their first manager, the self-styled 'teenage tycoon shit' Andrew Loog Oldham, who invented the snarling image for Mick, Keith and Brian that engulfed even quiet old Bill and poor, soulful Charlie. Far from being sworn foes and rivals, Beatles and Stones socialised, compared notes, commiserated, even staggered their record releases so as not to spoil one another's pitch.

Their dialogue with their listeners could not have been more different. The wonderful effects of Beatle music were often inadvertent, sparks accidentally struck between the inimical talents of Lennon and McCartney. Where The Beatles were poets in their own private firmament, The Stones were pamphleteers, exactly tuned to the moods and mutinies of the street. The songs Mick Jagger began to write with Keith Richards reflected the half-incredulous sneer of a generation for whom adult censure was changing to pandering and indulgence. Jagger's voice, in the quintessential Stones anthem, is riven with the delicious *angst* of finding the world too much at one's feet; the insufferable *ennui* of being handed everything. 'I can't get no. . . hey hey hey.'

Musically they have been much underestimated. Their founding spirit, Brian Jones, was a natural virtuoso whom even John Lennon held in unabashed awe. It was Brian who pioneered British Pop's use of arcane instruments like sitar, autoharp and African xylophone. Thanks mainly to him, the Stones' *Aftermath* album is a rough colour print of Swinging London, a year ahead of the Beatles' *Sgt Pepper*.

That year, 1966, was a crucial one in every way. It marked the major power-shift within The Stones, isolating Brian from the new songwriting axis of Mick and Keith. It also decided who was top dog in the recently named 'Style Capital of the World'. The Beatles, no longer a performing band, had fled to the suburbs to live as millionaire garden gnomes. The Stones had the freedom of the city and the key to the street.

They are integral to any vision of London in those new Arabian Nights. They are in the joss-scented boutiques, grabbing armfuls of clothes and hats and cloaks, with never a thought of payment. They are in the World's End pubs, the King's

Road bistros, the West End clubs with looking-glasses for doors. They are in the Queen Anne houses of socialites and trendy art-dealers, where coffee sugar tastes of LSD and marble Adam mantlepieces display interesting little piles of China snow. Think of anything that made the '66 In-Crowd. A black-windowed Austin Princess. A long-legged, blonde 'dolly bird' in marmalade fur. A wine-dark satin shirt with leg o' mutton sleeves. A hookah smouldering among Moroccan divans. The Stones rode in it, wolfed it, wore it, sprawled on it and smoked it. The Welsh actor Victor Spinetti — that least likely confidant of Sixties pop idols — remembers meeting them all in '66, on an early hookah-hookey to Marrakesh. Brian Jones, with his Afghan furs and angelic gold fringe, was suffering from a head cold. Spinetti good naturedly handed him a Beechams Powder. 'Hey, thanks man,' Brian gasped, slitting open the packet and inhaling the harmless remedy with one snort.

More crucially, their music and image shattered the caste system in British youth. Until then, Rock 'n' Roll had been viewed as dingily proletarian, the resort of labourers and Teddy Boys. The middle and upper classes clung to quiet and melody. Now, nothing could be more socially infra-dig than to like what had formerly been called a 'ballad'. Oxford undergrads and debutantes could be seen bopping wildly to unreformed Chicago Blues. The 'classless' revolution was under way.

In Mick Jagger was concentrated every paradox of the new order: a 'dirty', 'ugly' Pop star, vilified for the Art School frankness of his lyrics, who was nonetheless wooed by High Society, walked out with an Austrian baroness's daughter, lived graciously in Cheyne Walk and, against his slaveringly sexual stage persona, led the private life of a fastidious young college don. Small wonder that, when Society's indulgence of youth swung back again to furious disapproval, envy and vengefulness, there should have been only one possible scapegoat.

The setting-up of Jagger and Keith Richards by Fleet Street hand-in-hand with Scotland Yard remains the sourest repudiation of 1967 as a 'Summer of Love'. Scenes from their drugs trial should be compulsory viewing for anyone still cherishing the notion of British justice as fair and sensible. What to select from the general vista of malevolent asininity? The judicial witticisms of Judge Leslie Allen Block? The decision to parade Jagger in handcuffs like some eighteenth century sheep-stealer? The sniggering, among those allegedly concerned with public morality, over an officially concocted story that, when the police arrived at Keith Richards's house, Jagger was licking a Mars bar in Marianne Faithfull's vagina?

The hallucinating decade offered few climaxes more surreal than that following Jagger's release (in large part thanks to a *Times* leader by William Rees-Mogg) when wicked cunnilinguist suddenly found himself transformed into boy potentate, smoothed down by obsequious hands, placed in a helicopter and wafted to the twilit garden of Sir John Ruggles-Brise, there to preside at a symposium of civic and church leaders upon 'What the young people of Britain really want'. De Quincey, at his most besotted, can hardly have known a wilder trip. He was never again to be at a loss for words. I picture him most characteristically at that big New York press conference only a few weeks later: the master equivocator, in his skinny ice cream lapels, fielding another question from a tough woman journalist.

'Are you any more satisfied now than when you last came to the US?'

'D' you mean financially?' Jagger inquires with his opaque smile. 'Sexually? Philosophically?'

From there on, Stones mark every stage of an era struggling to keep love and peace alive as it declines inexorably towards chaos and murder. Remember 1969, when the sunshine over their Hyde Park half-million truly seemed to have become everlasting? Not to Brian Jones, exiled from the miracle he'd made and condemned to lonely death among the shades of Piglet and Winnie the Pooh. Not to Marianne Faithfull, whom domestic life with Jumping Jack Flash was already propelling towards her junkie's wall in Windmill Street. Not to Meredith Hunter, the black boy hacked to death on Altamont Raceway.

But The Stones had a good time.

So they did in the Seventies, into which they abseiled at the last moment, landing neatly on their feet. The ultimate group became the ultimate 'band', with all the new imagery that formerly workaday, unpretentious little word came to suggest. These were years when a 'band' required scaffolding towers to be built each side of it, searchlit Zeppelins to float overhead and the fearful, adoring efforts of hundreds of roadies and gofers to launch it into performance. They were years when a 'band' on tour enjoyed a lifestyle not seen since Ancient Rome under the nastier Augustans. They were years when a 'band' set the pattern for that parallel world of monster conceit, megalomania and kill-or-be-killed greed which, in its Seventies mid-season, Mick Jagger would so characteristically sum up as Only Rock 'n' Roll.

For me Only Rock 'n' Roll is epitomised by one occasion, circa 1976. The Stones are at a reception in a penthouse suite high above Hyde Park. A waiter approaches with a tray of expensive cocktails. One of the Stones' party seizes the tray and pitches it through an opening in the panoramic window. Another waiter appears with a fresh tray. This, too, is riotously grabbed from his hands and thrown after the first. It turns into a game of snatching trays of cocktails from waiters and flinging them out of the window. The Highballs, Manhattans, Tequila Sunrises and Bloody Marys vaporise like faint rainbows over the Hyde Park tree-tops. Yet again, The Stones are having a good time.

Paradoxically, it was in this season of their most heart-sinking self-indulgence and conceit that the Stones reached their musical apotheosis. It was the time when Mick was busy with Bianca and socialising and Keith took over direction of the group. It was the time of 'Honky-Tonk Woman', 'Tumbling Dice' and other pared-down classics built round lazy, lethal chord riffs that plunged the song into the bloodstream almost before Jagger could open his mouth. After *Aftermath*, the album that will endure is *Exile On Main Street*, Keith's tour de force from exile in Villefranche. (A legend persists to this day that power for the mobile studio was illicitly tapped from France's electric railway system.)

On they still rolled, an organism inwardly as elastic and compartmentalised as some amoeba seen under the microscope; healing over marks of chaos, casualties, even corpses left behind; now and then adding or subtracting a cell out on the periphery. The uncomfortable virtuosity of Mick Taylor came and went. The comfortable bum notes of Ronnie Wood made an excuse and stayed. Bill Wyman and Charlie Watts continued their marginal, nearly normal lives, uncomplainingly catching flak they had not merited. As all connected with it soon realised, the amoeba had but two vital features. There was its broad, sagging open mouth. And its multi-tracked, pumping right arm.

The Jagger-Richards partnership is, in human terms, more remarkable than that of Lennon and McCartney. Far more extreme opposites than John and Paul, apparently infuriated by almost every facet of one another, they have nonetheless kept themselves and an organisation together through crises and schisms that make The Beatles' break-up seem like a civilised goodbye.

That Jagger should be a fundamentally unattractive character is inevitable. What else could be expected in one who, from the age of twenty or so, has received flattery and cossetting like the Sun King? There is, indeed, much of a sawn-off Louis XIV about Jagger: his use of courtiers and ritual, his infinitesimal attention span, his insistence at the heart of his travelling Versailles that he is a simple man of simple tastes, indifferent to status or money. For all his wealth and fashionableness, the one thing he cannot seem to acquire is class. That he had only while married to Bianca. Recently, for complex reasons, I happened to be in a furniture warehouse as some of Bianca's clothes were disinterred from cardboard boxes where they had lain since the divorce. There was an odd sense of Tutankhamun's tomb in opening each carton of sumptuous Ossie Clark and Halston dresses worn by Bianca during her unhappy tenure as Mrs Jack Flash, mixed up with the exquisite little tweed coats she had tailored for their daughter, Jade. Whenever you came to something ratty — a sweat-dried jumpsuit or fringed buckskin coat — that was Mick's.

Keith, on the other hand, is as endearing a personality as ever lurked within the aspect of Count Dracula on a bad morning. Who, looking into that grave-hollowed face, would ever suspect quick wit, authentic humour or the boozy, affectionate voice of some old-time theatrical actor-manager? While Mick is an idol with more than one precedent — Valentino, Presley, James Brown — Keith's is a tattered profile utterly unique: the 'Human Riff', personification of self-ruin on epic scale, as spare and wickedly elegant as the lick he plays on Brown Sugar.

They bill themselves privately as 'The Glimmer Twins', and many say what has kept them together, albeit nagging like old marrieds, is the secret longing of each to emulate the other. Mick, for all his social ambitions, really would like something useful to do in the band. The 'Human Riff' is a thinker and wordsmith *manqué*, with no one to talk to but thick-eared bodyguards.

Weathering even Keith's heroically stupid Canadian heroin bust in '77, The Glimmer Twins kept it going over the threshold of another decade. There was that '81 World Tour, fuelled rather more by Jovan perfume sponsorship than by sulphurous energy, with Jagger, now a keep-fit fanatic in gussetted knee-breeches, pelting his audience with long-stemmed roses from a suspended cherry-picker crane. On which bizarre anticlimactic note we apparently said farewell to the World's Greatest Rock 'n' Roll Band.

The decade that followed was totally to transform, not merely the face and figure of Pop, but its place in society. What was once a secret password for youth became a fantasy for all age groups, the ad industry's kneejerk ruse to market anything from cat food to government policies. Pop musicians were pariahs no longer but respected figures in the Establishment. Sweatshirts and designer stubble became a uniform of conventionality almost equalling the City gent's rolled umbrella and bowler hat. Yesterday's outlaws were today's assiduous status seekers, applying for the Garrick or MCC, hunting with the Quorn or queuing up at white-tie galas to shake Princess Diana's hand.

In eight years, one would think, enough wild new sensations have come and gone to bury The Glimmer Twins for ever. There has been the spit-hurling punk energy of The Clash, The Damned and Squeeze. There has been the melodrama of Spandau Ballet and Ultravox, the Chaplinesque hyperactivity of Fun Boy 3 and Madness, the rag-tag transvestism of Culture Club, the double-shampooed glamour of Duran Duran, the minimalist chic of The Police. There has been the jazzy neurosis of Curiosity Killed the Cat, the good-humoured self-pity of Level 42, the sub-Byronic anguish of U2, the heavy metal burlesque of Bon Jovi and Def Leppard, the dole queue camp of Erasure and Simply Red, the white Motown trilling of Wet Wet Wet, the peroxide blandness of Bros. A hundred fresh hits bands with a thousand new ideas and a million new poses. But still, it seems, only one basic role-model.

For proof, go to any Pop concert, anywhere. See the audience kept waiting hour after hour, in the tradition established by Hyde Park and Altamont, thrilling under the faint lash of their idols' dilatoriness, indifference and contempt. Feel the great surge of sympathetic forgiveness as — with arms outspread in sarcastic brotherhood — the idols finally condescend to appear.

Watch the lead singer as he struts downstage, following a road already trodden out by hundreds in the footsteps of Mick Jagger. Notice how, as if following directions from a recipe book, he prances to and fro, changing hands on the mike at his mouth to lift a messianic arm and beckon down the screams. The advent of girl front-men has not helped the problem, which is basically that no toss of head, no grind of hips, no mince or flounce or backward fling of hair exists that wasn't registered twenty years ago as exclusive copyright of Jumping Jack Flash.

Examine the figures round about. . . the lead guitarist who would be Keith. . . the bass-player brooding like Bill. . . the drummer, hoping he smiles with Charlie's discreet charm. It's all still absolutely the latest thing.

Even the most original Pop attraction of the Eighties is at last authenticated merely in terms of Sixties *déjà vu.* After twenty years of unsuccessful aspirants, Michael Jackson truly can claim to have created excitement on a scale comparable with The Beatles. With the broadening of Jackson's appeal, there has arisen a scratchier, surlier flipside to the screams in Prince. Though names and complexions change, the same basic character difference remains. 'Are you Beatles or are you. . .'

As choice in the Pop hypermarket goes on doubling and redoubling, explain the ageless power of tracks, recorded on Neanderthal equipment two decades ago and more. Watch for a familiar moment in almost any disco night, when the pneumatic drilling of Rap subsides and the deejay puts on a single whose notoriety lingers on like a faint poltergeist in vinyl. See the dark chords swoop into every corner and bring their eternal crowd of transfixed zombies boogieing out under the lights. There still is no quicker way to wake the blood than that Frankenstein strut, with its voice, sneering from the silk-lined long ago. 'I can't get no. . . hey hey hey.'

Observe how, regularly every few years, the script Andrew Loog Oldham wrote a generation ago is replayed virtually word for word. See the same tale of make-believe wickedness and *ersatz* outrage spun around The Beastie Boys as was used to promote chart action for The Move, Slade, the Sex Pistols, Sigue Sigue Sputnik and Frankie Goes to Hollywood. Marvel how the same antique hype can still promote flurries in the tabloid press, calls for bans by turnip-headed MPs and denunciations from the pulpits of headline-hungry clergymen.

Watch the latest crew of bad lads sprawling on a sofa in a pose unhelpful to photographers, smoking, scowling and exulting in a wickedness that seems wholly original. Why is it one's thoughts so irresistibly turn back twenty years? To *Ready Steady Go* and *Sunday Night at the Palladium.* To Carnaby Street, Cheyne Walk and Chichester Assizes. To beggars' banquets, Pope, dead butterflies and what disgracefully delicious things can be accomplished with a Mars bar. . . .

It's The Rolling Stones. Then, now and for all time. Having a good time.

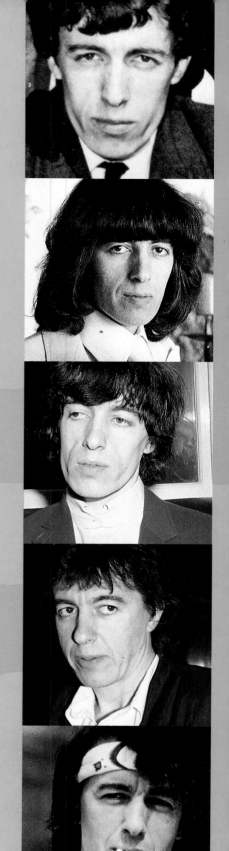

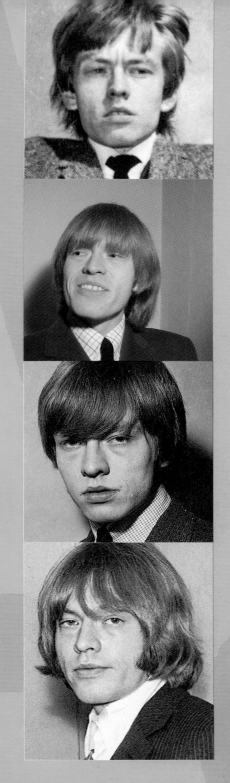

Dartford…

Cheltenham…

Bexleyheath…

Penge…

Sidcup…

Harrow…

Ealing…

Twickenham…

Kingston-on-Thames…

Eel Pie Island…

Richmond…

Soho

The early times

'We could use the group but not the singer.
He sounds too coloured.'
Producer, BBC Light Programme *Saturday Club*

1954

The future Glimmer Twins meet at Wentworth County Primary School, Dartford, Kent. Mick later recalled his first meeting with the nascent Human Riff: 'I asked him what he wanted to do when he grew up. He said he wanted to be a cowboy like Roy Rogers and play a guitar. I wasn't that impressed by Roy Rogers, but the bit about the guitar did interest me.'

They lost touch while Mick was at Dartford Grammar School, an apathetic pupil save in basketball (top row, right, in school team). His PE instructor father, Joe, wrote the definitive book on the sport and organised an early children's activity programme on television, in which Mick would demonstrate the right way to put up a tent or get into a canoe. His school friends even then noticed an aura of exclusivity.

Alexis Korner, father of the British Blues movement, who first collected the pebbles that would become The Stones. It was at Korner's club in Ealing, under an ABC teashop, that Mick and Keith first met 'Elmo Lewis', alias Brian Jones, brilliant slide guitarist and shameless fatherer of illegitimate babies.

Mick Jagger was singing with Korner's band, Blues Incorporated, when it was offered a nationwide broadcast, on the BBC Light Programme's *Jazz Club*. But the fee was not enough to include Jagger.

'Mick Jagger, R & B vocalist, is taking a rhythm and blues club into the Marquee tomorrow night while Blues Inc is doing its Jazz Club gig…the lineup is Jagger (vocals), Keith Richards, Elmo Lewis (guitars), Dick Taylor (bass), 'Stew' (piano), Mick Avory (drums).'

From *Jazz News*, July 11, 1962.

They are now Rolling Stones —occasionally Rollin' Stones— the name chosen by Brian in honour of Muddy Waters (left). Bill Wyman, né Perks, and Charlie Watts, formerly with Blues Incorporated, complete the ensemble of fill-in dogsbodies at the Soho Marquee Club. It still includes Ian Stewart (third from right), Blues pianist, racing cyclist and selfless provider of food and gas-meter shillings to Mick, Brian and Keith in their squalid Chelsea flat. In a few weeks, 'Stew' will be dropped from the lineup for looking 'too normal'. Asked to stay on as roadie and back-up pianist, he swallowed his pride and agreed. 'I thought, "I can't go back to working at ICI after this. I might as well stay with them and see the world." '

April 1962. Andrew Loog Oldham, ex-boutique assistant, failed Pop singer and inspirational media-manipulator, stumbles on The Stones playing in a room behind the Station Hotel, Richmond.

'I knew what I was looking at. It was sex. And I was forty-eight hours ahead of the pack.'

Oldham (right) had formerly worked for Beatles manager Brian Epstein (below left), to whom he was later to offer a half-share in The Stones. His exemplar as a manager was 'Wall of Sound' wizard Phil Spector (above left) from whom he borrowed dark glasses and the employment of ugly bodyguards with names like Reg The Butcher.

'As far as I'm concerned, when Keith sat in a corner and played those "Not Fade Away" chords, that was the first song The Stones ever wrote.' Andrew Loog Oldham

Their first single was a wishy-washy cover of Chuck Berry's 'Come On', their second a manic deconstruction of 'I Wanna Be Your Man', a handout from The Beatles. Not until they recorded Buddy Holly's 'Not Fade Away' could a distinctive note be heard.

Signed to Decca records by the A & R man who had previously let the Fab Four go to EMI... managed by an ex-associate of Brian Epstein... launched on the flood tide of international Beatlemania...what else could they have originally seemed but mere southern Mersey-beats?

Several weeks would pass, mutinously encased in uniform leather waistcoats and Beatle boots, before Andrew Loog Oldham had his Great Idea.

Worcester…

Wolverhampton…

Manchester…

Birmingham…

Glasgow…

Salisbury…

Ipswich…

Liverpool…

Paris…

New York…

Chicago…

Hollywood

The naughty times

'Would You Let Your Daughter Go With A Stone?'
Melody Maker headline,
suggested by Andrew Loog Oldham

1965

DON ARDEN ENTERPRIS

THE FABULOUS

EVERLY BROTHERS

THE

ROLLIN STONES

MICKIE MOST

☆ T

Compere: BOB BAI

LONDON, New Vic	Sun., Sept. 29th, 6.00 & 8.30		**DERBY**, Gaumont	Fri., Oct. 11	
STREATHAM, Odeon	Tues., Oct. 1st, 7.00 & 9.10		**DONCASTER**, Gaumont	Sat., Oct. 12	
EDMONTON, Regal	Wed., Oct. 2nd, 6.45 & 9.00		**LIVERPOOL**, Odeon	Sun., Oct. 13	
SOUTHEND, Odeon	Thur., Oct. 3rd, 6.45 & 9.00		**MANCHESTER**, Odeon	Wed., Oct. 16	
GUILDFORD, Odeon	Fri., Oct. 4th, 6.45 & 9.00		**GLASGOW**, Odeon	Thur., Oct. 17	
WATFORD, Gaumont	Sat., Oct. 5th, 6.15 & 8.45		**NEWCASTLE**, Odeon	Fri., Oct. 18	
CARDIFF, Capitol	Sun., Oct. 6th, 5.45 & 8.00		**BRADFORD**, Gaumont	Sat., Oct. 19	
CHELTENHAM, Odeon	Tues., Oct. 8th, 7.00 & 9.10		**HANLEY**, Gaumont	Sun., Oct. 2	
WORCESTER, Gaumont	Wed., Oct. 9th, 6.45 & 9.00		**SHEFFIELD**, Gaumont	Tues., Oct. 22	
WOLVERHAMPTON, Gaumont	Thur., Oct. 10th, 6.30 & 8.40		**NOTTINGHAM**, Odeon	Wed., Oct. 2	

S LTD. present

BO DIDDLEY

with

'THE DUCHESS' & JEROME

G

JULIE GRANT

E FLINTSTONES

6.30 & 8.45	BIRMINGHAM, Odeon	Thur., Oct. 24th.	6.45 & 9.00
6.15 & 8.30	TAUNTON, Gaumont	Fri., Oct. 25th.	7.00
5.40 & 8.00	BOURNEMOUTH, Gaumont	Sat.	
6.20 & 8.45	SALISBURY, Gaumo		
6.45 & 9.00	SOUTHAMPTON, Gau		
7.00 & 9.30	ST. ALBANS, Odeon		
6.20 & 8.45	LEWISHAM, Odeon		
6.15 & 8.30	ROCHESTER, Odeon		
6.30 & 8.45	IPSWICH, Gaumont		
6.15 & 8.30	HAMMERSMITH, Odeon		

September 1963. First big break, on nationwide package tour. The promoter, Don Arden, was famous in his day for hanging recalcitrant business associates out of his office-window by their ankles.

For The Stones, the great attraction was sharing a bill with their Rhythm and Blues idol, Bo Diddley. In homage, they dropped all Diddley numbers from their own stage performance.

The *New Musical Express* noted this extraordinary new group 'who often don't bother to change before they go on stage'. However, clean hair and pancake makeup remained *de rigueur*.

'The whole lot of you,' wrote one outraged parent, 'should be given a good bath and all that hair should be cut off. I'm not against Pop music when it's sung by a nice clean boy like Cliff Richard, but you are a disgrace. Your filthy appearance is likely to corrupt teenagers all over the country.'

At a school in Coventry, 11 boys were suspended for growing their hair as long as The Stones'. Their headmaster said they could return when it was 'cut neatly, like The Beatles'.

When Mick Jagger made a court appearance in Staffordshire on three minuscule motoring offences, his solicitor asked that the length of his hair should not count against him. 'The Duke of Marlborough had hair longer than my client, and he won several famous battles. His hair was powdered, I think, because of fleas. My client has no fleas.'

'They look like boys whom any self-respecting mum would lock in the bathroom,' said the *Daily Express*. 'But the Rolling Stones — five tough young London-based music-makers with doorstep mouths, pallid cheeks and unkempt hair — are not worried what mums think. For, now that the Beatles have registered with all age-groups, the Stones have taken over as the voice of the teens.'

Brian is still very much front man with his new blond Beatle mop and four inch collar. In the deal lately signed with agent Eric Easton, he has wangled £5 a week more than the others. Alexis Korner remembered how he always loved to see trouble start in the crowd — how he'd encourage it for all he was worth with goading shakes of his head or tambourine.

41

Choirboy innocent on the outside, Brian was a constant source of trouble within The Stones. The others mocked his superstar affectations, nicknaming him 'Mister Shampoo'. In those early days, before Mick and Keith's songwriting partnership, it was Brian's musicianship which gave the band its strength.

'Brian was a power within the Stones as long as he could pick up any instrument in the studio and get a tune out of it,' Andrew Loog Oldham says. 'As soon as he stopped trying and just played rhythm guitar, he was finished.'

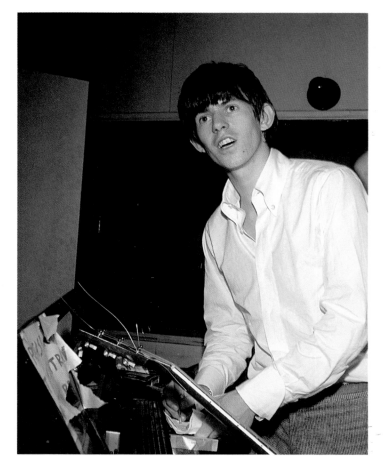

Few suspected the existence of their 'too normal' roadie, who uncomplainingly drove them, humped their gear and, after specially turbulent gigs, would go around the dressing-room handing out chips of wood, saying 'Here's what's left of your guitar...and here's what's left of your amp...'

Freak show on the road, 1964. Note outstanding examples of British *sang-froid,* front of picture, right.

To aircraft

Police protection, American style.
Some officers were not as mannerly
as these, demanding heavy backhanders
to prevent their charges being
torn limb from limb.

Chrissie Shrimpton, younger sister of famous model girl Jean, was Mick Jagger's first public girl friend. They met when The Stones were still cranking out Blues for suburban Surrey, and would have married but for Mick's wholly unexpected rise to Pop stardom.

Chrissie became a minor Swinging London celebrity, contributing a column to an American teen magazine, full of insights into their domestic life.

'Mick and I went down to visit George and Pattie Harrison last week… We sat in John's private cinema and watched a film called Citizen Kane… I think Stevie Winwood is the best singer we have. (Ouch! Mick has just hit me.)…'

The glowering Bailey chic of '64. Mick kept to the back, so as not to appear to benefit from being a friend of the photographer.

This was the image that shattered the caste system in British youth. Rock 'n' Roll graduated from proletarian dance halls to fashionable clubs. Debs and undergraduates bopped to unreformed Chicago Blues.

No greater difference existed between the Beatles and Stones than in their first choice of female friend. While the gauche northerners by and large picked local hairdressers or emptily pretty dolly birds, the worldly Londoners favoured a racier type altogether, exotic, sophisticated and their equal in mischief and adventurousness.

German fashion model Anita Pallenberg (right) is the woman who came closest to being a full-blooded Stone. Brian Jones's girl first, she switched to Keith — as many thought — with the ultimate aim of seducing Mick. It was she who persuaded the biddable Brian to pose in Nazi S.S. uniform, who created the near-fatal enmity between Mick and Keith and who encouraged the dangerous collective interest in Black Magic and the occult. By the end of the Sixties, many in the Stones circle believed she was a witch. 'I often used to think,' Marianne Faithfull says, 'that if one spent the evening with Anita, one could very easily get killed.'

Marianne (left) was the daughter of an Austrian baroness and an English academic, raised in Reading near the biscuit factory, schooled at a strict convent, her life as sunny and pretty as a girl in a Renoir. All was to change on the day she met Andrew Loog Oldham and through him, her future lover, supporter and destroyer, Mick Jagger.

AFTE
-MATI

April 1966. Their fourth album — originally titled *Can You Walk On The Water* — brings near creative parity with their Liverpool rivals. All 14 tracks are Jagger-Richards gems, like 'Under My Thumb', 'Out Of Time', 'Lady Jane' and 'Mother's Little Helper'. Brian's instrumental virtuosity is at full strength, on sitar, flute, autoharp and marimba. The result is a rough colour print of Swinging London a year ahead of The Beatles' Sgt. Pepper. One can almost see King's Road on a Saturday morning, the white Courrèges boots, the bistros and bric-à-brac.

1965. Andrew Loog Oldham hands over management of himself and his empire—including The Stones—to Allen Klein, the New York accountant and entrepreneur. For Klein it is a stepping-stone to his ultimate objective The Beatles, whom he will annexe four years later, with eternally debatable results.

As Oldham later recounted it, Klein's overtures to him had classic simplicity. Klein: 'Andrew, whaddaya want?' Oldham: 'I want a Rolls Royce.' Klein: 'You got it.'

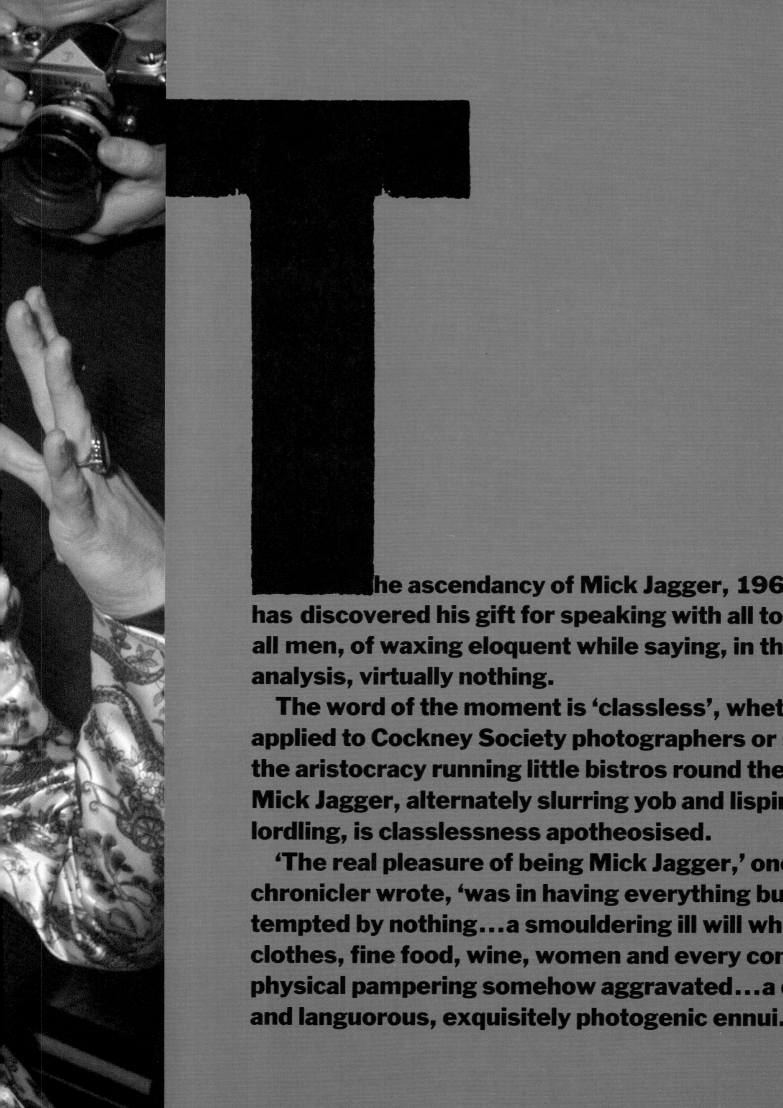

The ascendancy of Mick Jagger, 1966. He has discovered his gift for speaking with all tongues to all men, of waxing eloquent while saying, in the last analysis, virtually nothing.

The word of the moment is 'classless', whether applied to Cockney Society photographers or sprigs of the aristocracy running little bistros round the corner. Mick Jagger, alternately slurring yob and lisping lordling, is classlessness apotheosised.

'The real pleasure of being Mick Jagger,' one chronicler wrote, 'was in having everything but being tempted by nothing…a smouldering ill will which silk clothes, fine food, wine, women and every conceivable physical pampering somehow aggravated…a drained and languorous, exquisitely photogenic ennui.'

Chelsea...

West Wittering...

Tangier...

Wormwood Scrubs...

Hyde Park...

Rio...

Marrakesh...

Chichester...

Brixton...

New York...

San Francisco...

Altamont

The punishing times

'It's an ordinary day for Brian.
Like, he died every day, you know.'
Pete Townshend

1966

New York

HAVE YOU SEEN YOUR MOTHER, BABY?

(Just to put Ed Sullivan's mind at rest.)

Flower Power breaks out in The Stones — though for these half-hearted hippies, the Love and Peace era will be more largely reckonable in terms of courts and police. They will shortly reach their musical nadir with the wishy-washy *Satanic Majesties* album. They will sing 'We Love You' as a sarcastic valentine to the Establishment which has lately clapped two of them into jail.

The main interest of the picture is Brian's almost uncanny resemblance to Patricia Hayes as 'Edna The Inebriate Woman'.

1967. Half-cock hippies try to do their Sgt. Pepper thing. To be fair, given the outside pressures, it's miraculous any finished album emerged.

Their Satanic Majesties Request marks The Stones' creative nadir and the exit of Andrew Loog Oldham as manager.

'It ended up as a real patchwork,' Keith Richards said later. 'Half of it was "Let's give the people what we think they want." The other half was "Let's get out of here as quickly as possible."'

When the going was good for 'Mick and Lady Faithfull,' as the Blue Mink song characterised them. Marianne, a true intellectual, took Mick's education in hand, telling him what books to read, introducing him to the theatre, opera and ballet, filling his house in Cheyne Walk with grand antiques. 'Look at that!' Mick would exclaim, pointing upward at a chandelier. 'Six thousand quid for a fuckin' light!'

The gifted journalist Gina Richardson, who visited them in early '69, noted the harmony and humour of the relationship. Her only caveat was Mick's habit of slopping around in mules like a slatternly housewife. 'They seemed,' she wrote, 'like two children left in charge of the house while the grown ups are out.'

The fatal threesome that took the road to Morocco, Spring 1967.

They drove in Keith's Bentley Continental, nicknamed 'The Blue Lena'; Brian and Anita lounging in the back like blond, fur-wrapped Borgias, Keith upfront, laughing at Tom Keylock the chauffeur's Cockney patter.

All went well until Toulon, where Brian developed a high fever and was admitted to hospital with suspected pneumonia.

He insisted that Keith and Anita should continue the journey together. He'd take a plane later and meet them in Tangier. . .

Mick Jagger, photographed in Tangier by Cecil Beaton, Spring 1967.

The illustrious chronicler of Royalty and the pre-war *belle époque* was an exotic addition to the party which had fled to Morocco after the police invasion of Keith Richard's house. Beston's diaries record coming upon 'a sleepy group of gipsies… Brian Jones with his girl-friend Anita Pallenberg — dirty white face, dirty blackened eyes, dirty canary drops of hair, barbaric jewellery — Keith Richard in eighteenth-century suit, long black coat and the tightest pants… Mick very gentle with perfect manners. He has much appreciation and his small, albino-fringed eyes notice everything.'

Beaton was absorbed into a circle that included Michael Cooper the photographer, Robert Fraser, the gallery owner nabbed with Mick and Keith, and Brion Gysin the *avant-garde* painter. There were shopping raids, Moroccan banquets (Mick as ever a reliable trencherman) and LSD trips to the sound of Elmore James Blues. Brian took out his deepening insecurity and isolation within the band by beating up Anita in their hotel room.

Cecil Beaton's sharp sense picked up the general air of indecision and lassitude. 'No one could make up their minds what to do, or when.' He also noticed the cheap shoddiness of Pop star finery.

Jagger he found a natural model, though — especially on mornings after — far from conventionally beautiful. 'The very strong sun reflected from white ground, made his face look a podgy, shapeless mass; eyes very small, nose very pink, hair sandy dark. He is sexy, yet completely sexless. He could nearly be a eunuch.'

The basking noonday face betrays nothing of the turmoil happening out of shot. Anita is about to ditch Brian and take off with Keith in his Rolls Royce, 'the Blue Lena.' In not too many weeks — chivalrously taking the rap for Marianne — Mick himself will be paraded before the British public, handcuffed like some eighteenth-century convict.

THE TIMES

PRINTING HOUSE SQUARE, LONDON, E.C.4. TELEPHONE: 01-236 2000

WHO BREAKS A BUTTERFLY ON A WHEEL?

MR. JAGGER has been sentenced to imprisonment for three months. He is appealing against conviction and sentence, and has been granted bail until the hearing of the appeal later in the year. In the meantime, the sentence of imprisonment is bound to be widely discussed by the public. And the circumstances are sufficiently unusual to warrant such discussion in the public interest.

MR. JAGGER was charged with being in possession of four tablets containing amphetamine sulphate and methyl amphetamine hydrochloride; these tablets had been bought, perfectly legally, in Italy, and brought back to this country. They are not a highly dangerous drug, or in proper dosage a dangerous drug at all. They are of the benzedrine type and the Italian manufacturers recommend them both as a stimulant and as a remedy for travel sickness.

In Britain it is an offence to possess these drugs without a doctor's prescription. MR. JAGGER'S doctor says that he knew and had authorized their use, but he did not give a prescription for them as indeed they had already been purchased. His evidence was not challenged. This was therefore an offence of a technical character, which before this case drew the point to public attention any honest man might have been liable to commit. If after his visit to the POPE the ARCHB SHOP of CANTERBURY had bought proprietary airsickness pills on Rome airport, and imported the unused tablets into Britain on his return, he would have risked committing precisely the same offence. No one who has ever travelled and bought proprietary drugs abroad can be sure that he has not broken the law.

JUDGE BLOCK directed the jury that the approval of a doctor was not a defence in law to the charge of possessing drugs without a prescription, and the jury convicted. MR. JAGGER was not charged with complicity in any other drug offence that occurred in the same house. They were separate cases, and no evidence was produced to suggest that he knew that MR. FRASER had heroin tablets

or that the vanishing MR. SNEIDERMANN had cannabis resin. It is indeed no offence to be in the same building or the same company as people possessing or even using drugs, nor could it reasonably be made an offence. The drugs which MR. JAGGER had in his possession must therefore be treated on their own, as a separate issue from the other drugs that other people may have had in their possession at the same time. It may be difficult for lay opinion to make this distinction clearly, but obviously justice cannot be done if one man is to be punished for a purely contingent association with someone else's offence.

We have, therefore, a conviction against MR. JAGGER purely on the ground that he possessed four Italian pep pills, quite legally bought but not legally imported without a prescription. Four is not a large number. This is not the quantity which a pusher of drugs would have on him, nor even the quantity one would expect in an addict. In any case MR. JAGGER'S career is obviously one that does involve great personal strain and exhaustion; his doctor says that he approved the occasional use of these drugs, and it seems likely that similar drugs would have been prescribed if there was a need for them. Millions of similar drugs are prescribed in Britain every year, and for a variety of conditions.

One has to ask, therefore, how it is that this technical offence, divorced as it must be from other people's offences, was thought to deserve the penalty of imprisonment. In the courts at large it is most uncommon for imprisonment to be imposed on first offenders where the drugs are not major drugs of addiction and there is no question of drug traffic. The normal penalty is probation, and the purpose of probation is to encourage the offender to develop his career and to avoid the drug risks in the future. It is surprising therefore that JUDGE BLOCK should have decided to sentence MR. JAGGER to imprisonment, and particularly surprising as MR. JAGGER'S is about as mild a drug case as can ever have been brought before the Courts.

It would be wrong to speculate on the JUDGE'S reasons, which we do not know. It is, however, possible to consider the public reaction. There are many people who take a primitive view of the matter, what one might call a pre-legal view of the matter. They consider that MR. JAGGER has "got what was coming to to him". They resent the anarchic quality of the Rolling Stones' performances, dislike their songs, dislike their influence on teenagers and broadly suspect them of decadence, a word used by MISS MONICA FURLONG in the *Daily Mail*.

As a sociological concern this may be reasonable enough, and at an emotional level it is very understandable, but it has nothing at all to do with the case. One has to ask a different question: has MR. JAGGER received the same treatment as he would have received if he had not been a famous figure, with all the criticism and resentment his celebrity has aroused? If a promising undergraduate had come back from a summer visit to Italy with four pep pills in his pocket would it have been thought right to ruin his career by sending him to prison for three months? Would it also have been thought necessary to display him handcuffed to the public?

There are cases in which a single figure becomes the focus for public concern about some aspect of public morality. The Stephen Ward case, with its dubious evidence and questionable verdict, was one of them, and that verdict killed STEPHEN WARD. There are elements of the same emotions in the reactions to this case. If we are going to make any case a symbol of the conflict between the sound traditional values of Britain and the new hedonism, then we must be sure that the sound traditional values include those of tolerance and equity. It should be the particular quality of British justice to ensure that MR. JAGGER is treated exactly the same as anyone else, no better and no worse. There must remain a suspicion in this case that MR. JAGGER received a more severe sentence than would have been thought proper for any purely anonymous young man.

The '67 Summer of Love' reaches its apogee.

Les Perrin, the chain-smoking Fleet Street publicist whose presence Jagger had so much cause to bless.

The hallucinating decade offered few climaxes more bizarre than that following the quashing of Mick Jagger's prison sentence, when he appeared in a Granada TV *World In Action* special, debating morality and politics with the editor of *The Times*, William Rees-Mogg, former Home Secretary Lord Stow Hill, the Bishop of Woolwich and Jesuit Father Thomas Corbishley.

William Rees-Mogg's leader in his own paper —

headed with Pope's line 'Who breaks a butterfly on a wheel?' — had drawn national attention to Jagger's disgraceful treatment, despite a risk of prosecution for contempt of court.

This was Mick Jagger's moment of supreme triumph. The society which had mocked, abused and finally tried to destroy him, now cast itself down before him with all the apologetic reverence due to a misjudged Messiah. The editor, the peer, the bishop and the Jesuit earnestly entreated him to reveal 'what the young people in this country really think'. (And did he tell them? Of course not.)

The launch was a banquet at the Queensgate Hotel — attended by dignitaries such as Britain's US Ambassador-elect, Lord Harlech — which, in a very few minutes, dissolved into a schoolboy food-fight. The demented figure in top hat is Brian Jones, just after slamming a custard pie into Mick Jagger's face with what bystanders agreed was somewhat excessive force.

Over leaf: The original *Beggars Banquet* artwork, to which everyone so inexplicably objected. Inset: Decca Records chief Sir Edward Lewis. Not, by any stretch of the imagination, a street fightin' man.

December 1968. The Stones' greatest album finally makes it to the shops in a sleeve of irony-laden good taste.

Rolling Stones
Beggars Banquet

R. S. V. P.

December 1968. The Rolling Stones Rock and Roll Circus is filmed as a BBC TV Christmas special, featuring John and Yoko, The Who and Jethro Tull, plus Blues singer Taj Mahal, concert pianist Julius Katchen, model Donyal Luna, underground hero Ken Kesey and a supporting bill of jugglers, lion-tamers and clowns.

It has not been broadcast to this day.

84

Filming *Performance,* October 1968.

The movie — intended to be a happy-go-lucky Pop pic like *A Hard Day's Night* — cast Jagger as Turner, a reclusive Pop star, and Anita Pallenberg as his girl friend. One scene required them to make love in a threesome with an androgynous French girl in a carved and canopied antique bed.

'Anita didn't help Keith's insecurity,' Donald Cammell, the scriptwriter and co-director, remembers. 'She seemed to be teasing him about wanting Mick the way she used to tease Brian about wanting Keith. While we were filming, Keith never came near the set. He'd sit in the car outside and send in messages.'

June 1969
It is announced that Brian has quit the Stones because of 'disagreements over musical policy'

The end draws near for Brian Jones. Ousted from leadership of The Stones and ditched by Anita, he slides into a fog of booze, pills and alienating self-pity. As an almost willing sacrifice to the police drug squad, he is a jinx on the band's whole commercial future. There is no alternative but to fire him. On the night of July, 2, 1969, he is found dead in the swimming pool at his country house in Sussex. By a wholly typical bilious irony, the place formerly belonged to A. A. Milne, creator of Winnie the Pooh. Brian's last moments — shrouded in mystery to this day — are in a garden full of whimsical memorials to Pooh, Eeyore and Piglet.

Drama of pop guitarist

.30 am LATEST

BRIAN JONES 'STONES' FOUND DEAD

DON SHORT

Brian Jones, who quit the
last month, was found

d by friends who called at the
Body found by

friends

Stones came in a sudden
announcement last month.
He said: "The Stones' music is
not to my taste any more. I want
to play my own kind of music.

Peace, peace! He is not dead,
he doth not sleep.
He hath awakened from the
dream of life.
Tis we who, lost in stormy
visions, keep
With phantoms an
unprofitable strife.

Brian's replacement, twenty year-old Mick Taylor — formerly of John Mayall's Bluesbreakers — is shown to the world's press on the eve of the Hyde Park free concert that will do double duty as Brian's Requiem.

Taylor joins merely as a salaried sidesman, at £150 per week, in order to bring the band to full strength for its next US tour. He is a youth of almost painful innocence, a non-drinking, non-smoking macrobiotic vegetarian. Many changes are in store for him.

**'Now listen . . . cool it for a minute.
I'd just like to say something about Brian . . .
about how we feel about him just goin'
when we didn't expect it.'**

Hyde Park, July 5, 1969

The end of the affair looms for Mick and Marianne. Driven to despair by his infidelities and superstar remoteness, she has found solace in substances far more lethal than the cannabis in this famous bust.

'The worst thing about being with Mick was this rule he laid down that you must never show emotion in case people realised you weren't cool. Over the months, everything used to get bottled up inside me. I remember, on one of those holidays with everyone in Morocco, being in the middle of the Atlas Mountains and suddenly bursting into tears.'

The girl in the Renoir cornfield was now *Girl On A Motorcycle* in Roger Vadim's current schlock thriller.

Daily Mirror

5d.   Thursday, May 29, 1969   No. 20,348

Detectives swoop on pop singers' home

JAGGER AND MARIANNE CHARGED BY DRUG SQUAD

By HAROLD WHITTALL and RONALD RICKETTS

ROLLING STONES singer Mick Jagger and his girl friend Marianne Faithfull were arrested by drug squad detectives at their Chelsea home last night.

The couple were charged with having cannabis and will appear at Marlborough-street magistrates' court today.

The police raid on their home in Cheyne Walk, overlooking the Thames, was headed by Detective Sergeant Robin Constable, attached to Chelsea police station.

He talked to Jagger and Miss Faithfull while other detectives searched the premises. Substances were taken from the house for laboratory examination.

Then the two singers went to the police station.

There 25-year-old Jagger was charged in the name of Michael Philip Jagger.

Miss Faithfull, 22, was charged in her married name of Dunbar.

They were released on £50 bail each and returned home.

Velvet

Later Jagger, looking tired and wearing a pink velvet suit, stood on the doorstep and talked about the arrest

He said: "The police —about six or seven of them—arrived just after Marianne and I had finished our tea.

"They took us down to the police station.

"We went in my own car, not a police car."

Later the couple left their home, got into a car and drove off.

Jagger shouted from the car: "I am going to work now—we are going to the recording studios."

Miss Faithfull married artist John Dunbar in 1965. Divorce proceedings started last October.

A £500,000 JACKPOT FOR THE POOLS

By LONGSIGHT, Mirror Pools Expert

A NEW football pools scheme could bring £500,000 jackpots next season.

Punters will find it harder to win, but dividends will be bigger.

All of the big six pool companies except Littlewoods have scrapped the old Treble Chance system under which punters scored three points for a drawn match.

In its place comes the new deal. Punters will now get three points for a drawn match in which goals are scored, two points for a goalless draw, one point for an away or home win and two for a void match.

Littlewoods will run their old-style Treble Chance as well as the points-for-goals pools.

The biggest first dividend paid out on a single coupon so far is £338,000. That was in 1966.

The new scheme was announced by the Pools Promoters Association in London yesterday.

Littlewoods director Nigel Moores said: "This means bigger dividends. I think it is possible that we shall see a half-million-pound winner next season."

The joint chairman of Vernons Pools, Mr. George Kennerley, said: "This change was inevitable due to the pattern of football now being played."

Harder

"There have been on average fourteen draws a week and this is not good for the great glamour wins one associates with the pools.

"This new deal will make it harder for punters to win — but when they do they will win big."

The pools promoters blame modern Soccer for the lack of recent big winners.

In a statement they said: "Treble Chance dividends have been disappointingly low in recent seasons.

"The increase of defensive tactics in football often results in an abundance of drawn games."

A night out at the opera

Jagger and Marianne Faithfull, pictured on a visit to the opera at Covent Garden. As usual, they were dressed in colourful gear.

DJ John Peel says on the radio: I had VD

By RICHARD STOTT

CONTROVERSIAL disc jockey John Peel shocked radio listeners last night by admitting that he contracted venereal disease earlier this year.

Peel's admission came during a discussion about VD on his hour-long Radio One pop programme.

He said: "While we are being frankly honest, I contracted it myself at the beginning of this year for the first time.

"I am twenty-nine and did not know what was happening because the school I went to was one of those places which even to mention this disease would probably mean a beating."

Amazed

Angry listeners rang the BBC to complain about Peel's "confession."

One said: "I was amazed when he came out with his admission. I would have thought it was the kind of thing that he would want to keep to himself."

A BBC spokesman said: "We have had some calls about this. This was an ad lib show and Mr. Peel was talking seriously about a serious subject."

After the programme John Peel said: "I have no regrets for saying what I did. I didn't plan to mention it but it seemed to flow quite naturally as part of the conversation."

Storm

Liverpool-born Peel, darling of the "way out" pop world, was at the centre of a storm over remarks made about Premier Harold Wilson by satirist John Wells on Peel's "Night Ride" show last year.

This resulted in the BBC apologising to Mr. Wilson.

A month later Peel was attacked by a Baptist minister who accused his show of providing "filth, the like of which I have never heard before."

Vignette from the ghastly free festival on Altamont raceway in December, 1969. A young black spectator was later knifed to death a few yards from The Stones as they played.

A Hell's Angel 'steward' spoke eloquently for the new decade about to dawn:

'I ain't no peace creep, man. Ain't nobody goin' to get my bike, man. Anyone tries that, they gonna get got. And they *got* got.'

St Tropez…

Villefranche…

Geneva…

Montreux…

Knebworth…

Toronto…

Bel Air…

Montauk…

The Loire Valley…

Mustique

The one
too many times

'My marriage ended on my wedding day.'
Bianca Jagger

Corporate life begins with *Sticky Fingers*, the first album on The Rolling Stones' own label. Andy Warhol designed both the album-sleeve whose fly could be unzipped and the symbol of The Lapping Tongue.

'Brown Sugar' is the album's stickiest treat, fusing Keith's classic riff with Jagger's hip-shaking Dixie drawl in a paean of racist sexism that could have been about brown Mexican heroin or the Mars bar trick with a compliant plantation slave.

Jagger in the early Seventies, still at the apotheosis. 'No one else could portray that dancing paradox of athlete and stripper, that perpetual indecision between predatory satyr and timid, glitter-eyed faun.'

Enter The Girl
Without A Name, alias
Nicaraguan-born Bianca
Pérez Mora Macias.
Narcissus looked into
the mirror and was lost.

Their wedding in St
Tropez was a Rock 'n'
Roll Circus that shocked
Bianca. She would later
tell friends that her
marriage had ended on
her wedding day.

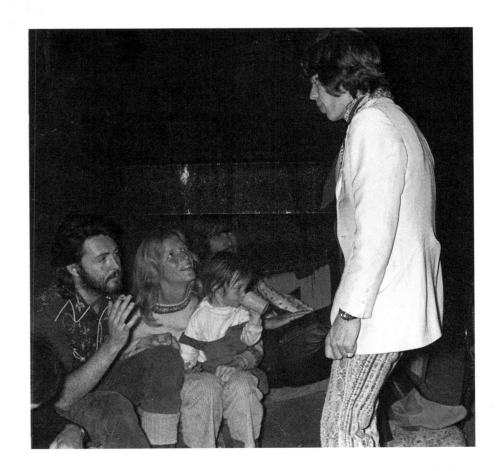

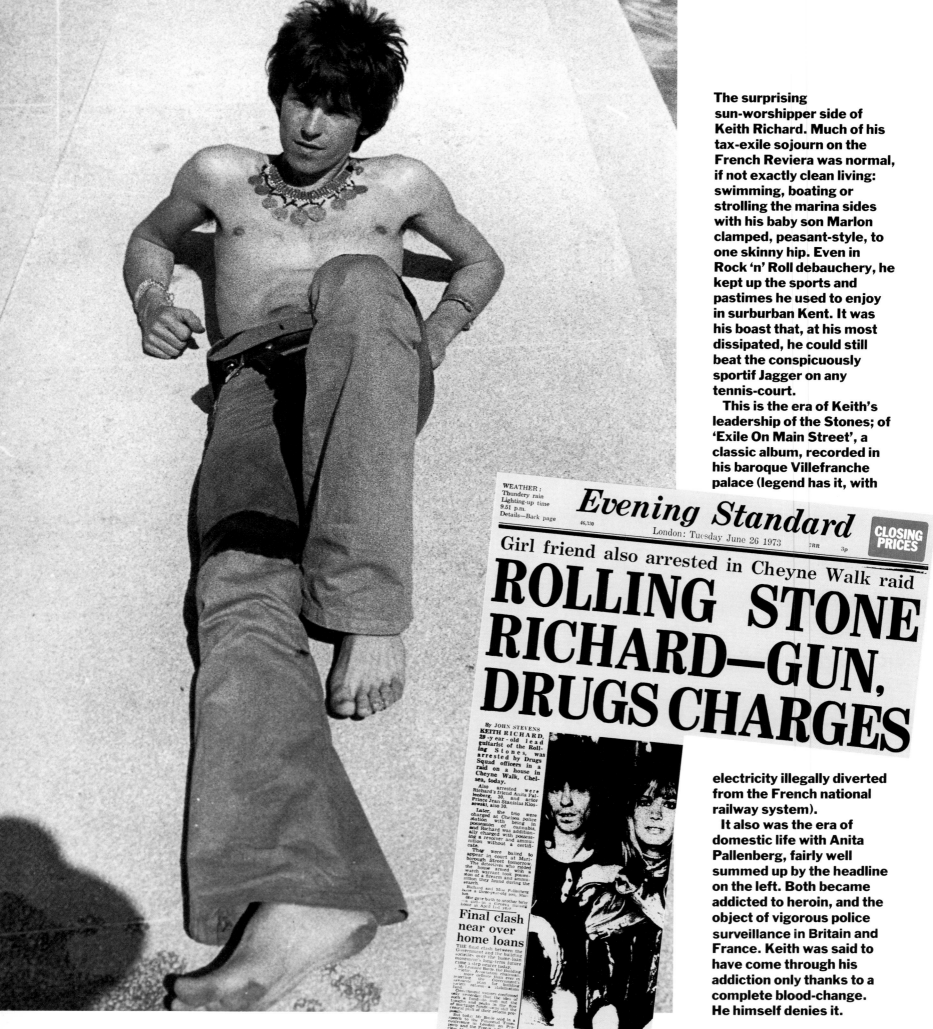

The surprising sun-worshipper side of Keith Richard. Much of his tax-exile sojourn on the French Reviera was normal, if not exactly clean living: swimming, boating or strolling the marina sides with his baby son Marlon clamped, peasant-style, to one skinny hip. Even in Rock 'n' Roll debauchery, he kept up the sports and pastimes he used to enjoy in surburban Kent. It was his boast that, at his most dissipated, he could still beat the conspicuously sportif Jagger on any tennis-court.

This is the era of Keith's leadership of the Stones; of 'Exile On Main Street', a classic album, recorded in his baroque Villefranche palace (legend has it, with electricity illegally diverted from the French national railway system).

It also was the era of domestic life with Anita Pallenberg, fairly well summed up by the headline on the left. Both became addicted to heroin, and the object of vigorous police surveillance in Britain and France. Keith was said to have come through his addiction only thanks to a complete blood-change. He himself denies it.

WEATHER:
Thundery rain
Lighting-up time
9.51 p.m.
Details—Back page

46,330

Evening Standard

London: Tuesday June 26 1973   7RR   3p

CLOSING PRICES

Girl friend also arrested in Cheyne Walk raid

ROLLING STONE RICHARD—GUN, DRUGS CHARGES

By JOHN STEVENS

KEITH RICHARD, 29-year-old lead guitarist of the Rolling Stones, was arrested by Drugs Squad officers in a raid on a house in Cheyne Walk, Chelsea, today.

Also arrested were Richard's friend Anita Pallenberg, 30, and actor Prince Jean Stanislas Klossowski, also 30.

Later, the trio were charged at Chelsea police station with being in possession of cannabis, and Richard was additionally charged with possessing a revolver and ammunition without a certificate.

They were bailed to appear in court at Marlborough Street tomorrow.

The detectives who raided the house, armed with a search warrant took possession of a firearm and ammunition they found during the search.

Richard and Miss Pallenberg have a three-year-old son, Marlon.

She gave birth to another baby — a girl — on the Reviera, nursing home in April last year.

Final clash near over home loans

THE final clash between the Government and the building societies over the home loan movement's long-term future came a step nearer today.

Mr Leonard Boyle, the Building Societies Association chairman, is more definite than ever in rejecting the Government's immediate plan for building society interest rates.

Government sources confirmed only yesterday that the idea of such a fund—to iron out increases and cuts in the flow of mortgage funds—was still the centre of their reform programme.

But today, Mr Boyle said in a speech to the Financial Times conference in London on Property and the Future, it appears clear to us the ... stabilisation fund will not work ...

KEITH RICHARD and Anita Pallenberg—they appear ... court tomorrow.

'I know,
it's only Rock 'n' Roll.
But I like it. Yes I do.'

At the height of mid-seventies high camp.

The road organisation now involved thirteen articulated trucks and one hundred and fifty tons of lights. The stage was an enormous flower whose bulletproof petals unfurled to reveal the 'band'. Additional props included a gigantic rubber phallus for Jagger to punch and pummel as he sang 'Star Star'.

Bianca at one of the least glamorous moments of her marriage. Mick's tax situation condemned them to fretful wanderings back and forth across the Atlantic, never making the settled home for which Bianca's conventional nature yearned. Isolated within The Stones organisation (which she called 'the Nazi State') she ultimately found herself obliged to compete for Mick's attention like any other courtier.

1974. Mick Taylor, the former non-smoking vegetarian, realises he must run for his life. The press release says he is quitting The Stones for 'a change of scene'.

The names of a dozen guitar virtuosi are mooted as successors, among them Jimmy Page, Peter Frampton, Jeff Beck, Rory Gallagher, Shuggie Otis and Chris Spedding. The choice is Ronnie Wood, formerly of Rod Stewart's Faces.

'Woody' might have played more bum notes than any guitarist in British Rock. But his hair was spiky. His wrists were bangly. He would be a sidekick for Keith. He fitted.

Jerry Hall, the Texas truck-driver's daughter who won Mick Jagger, not only with her equine beauty but also her rumbustious humour and large separate income from international fashion modelling.

Before Jagger's advent, Jerry had been seeing Bryan Ferry of Roxy Music. When Ferry heard of their liaison, he said he was going to find Jagger and punch him. Friends dissuaded him by pointing out that Jagger currently looked extremely fit and might give back as good as he got. Ferry accepted the situation, settling down to the run of dirge-like, self-pitying singles that continue to this day.

Jerry later remarked what a far nicer person Mick had been to take down and meet the folks. When he saw a cockroach, he didn't flinch.

'This could be the last time. I don't know.'

February 1977. The Stones come near to splitting under the weight of Keith's most serious drugs bust. Mick abandons his Glimmer Twin in Toronto facing the prospect of a life prison sentence. To add to the chaos, Margaret Trudeau, wife of Canada's Prime Minister, has reportedly been seen in The Stones' hotel 'partying' in only a bathrobe.

1981. BACK W

VENGEANCE

THE NEW DEC

'IF YOU START

BABY, I WILL

TH A
N
ADE.

Jagger reborn as keep-fit fanatic for the Tattoo You tour in 1981. No longer a satin jumpsuit split to the pubis, but US football player's breeches with knee-pads and rigid front gusset. And nothing to drink onstage but mineral water.

ME UP . . .
NEVER STOP.'

Stones in the late Eighties, gathering moss at last.

Jagger now styles himself a 'dilettante Englishman', flitting among the world's fashion spots with his array of beautiful daughters by three different women. Solo recording success has, however, continued to elude him. The nearest was his 'Dancing In The Street' duet with David Bowie.

    Keith — now married to US model Pattie Hanson — appeared on film with Chuck Berry, valiantly trying to provide that Rock 'n' Roll Scrooge with a quality backing band.

    Charlie Watts returned to Jazz, his first love, forming a big band to play a season at Ronnie Scott's Club.

    Ronnie Wood exhibited his paintings.

    Spitting Image took the piss.

Who would have guessed it? Bill Wyman, the sexiest Stone of the late Eighties! And each one of those 1,000 conquests, apparently, is listed on his computer. A good decade for the most barely animate Stone, both in personal column inches and chart action. In 1981, he actually had a solo hit single. Rather more than can be said for the other person in this fraternal study.

Stop Press, March 1989:
Bill announces he will wed Mandy

THE STAR

THE FACTS NOT THE FICTION   MONDAY, AUGUST 4, 1986   **18p** (19p Cls)

Bears' picnic
SEE PAGE 27

STONE IN SEX PROBE OVER GIRL OF 13

Wyman with Mandy . . . she claims they lived together as man and wife

EXCLUSIVE

MY 1,000 WOMEN — By BILL WYMAN

SEE CENTRE PAGES

By BILL AKASS

Gymslip love claim

POLICE were last night investigating claims that Rolling Stone Bill Wyman had a love affair with a 13-year-old schoolgirl.

Detectives were studying reports that beautiful blonde Mandy Smith lost her virginity to the rock star, who will be 50 in October.

Mandy turned 16 just over a fortnight ago. She now lives in Spain with a new boyfriend.

Scotland Yard said yesterday: "We are aware of the report and are studying it closely. It is too early to say whether we will want to interview Mr Wyman."

The Yard said criminal charges relating to under-age sex are usually based on the evidence of the girl involved, or relatives.

It could also be brought to the attention of the police by "other parties."

Mandy claims that the 2½-year affair began after she met Wyman at a trendy disco. She alleges she lived with him as man and wife, doing the housework and sharing his bed.

Furious

She says she often met him from school, still wearing her uniform, and they jetted off for secret holidays together.

Mandy claims she ditched Wyman recently after falling in love with Irishman Keith Daley. She says her mother Pat knew of the affair with the star, who has a son four years older than Mandy.

Mandy's grandfather, Paddy Harris, 72, said he was angry about the affair, but he would not be making any complaints to the police. "It is up to the mother and father to take action if they want to," he added.

Wyman is furious that Mandy has broken his love code of silence, writes GEOFF BAKER.

Although he has had hundreds of lovers, none has spilled the beans before.

But in an exclusive interview with me, he admitted he had

Turn to Page 2 Col 5

**For God's sake
don't mention how
old we are.**

PICTURE CREDITS